GOOD EVENING EUROPE!

An Hachette UK Company
www.hachette.co.uk

First published in Great Britain in 2023 by Pyramid,
an imprint of Octopus Publishing Group Ltd
Carmelite House, 50 Victoria Embankment, London EC4Y 0DZ
www.octopusbooks.co.uk

ISBN 978-0-7537-3536-7

A CIP catalogue record for this book is available from the British Library

Printed and bound in Czech Republic

10 9 8 7 6 5 4 3 2 1

Publisher: Lucy Pessell
Designer: Isobel Platt
Editor: Feyi Oyesanya
Assistant Editor: Samina Rahman
Production Manager: Emily Noto

Picture credits: **Getty Images:** Anax/Bloomberg 68; Johannes Simon 69;
Jonathan Nackstrand/AFP 70; Sean Gallup 66; Sven Nackstrand/AFP 67;
Shutterstock: 65.

GOOD EVENING EUROPE!

AN UNOFFICIAL PARTY GUIDE FOR EVERY EUROVISION FAN

TRINITY ROUGÉ

CONTENTS

INTRODUCTION

The Eurovision Song Contest is the longest running TV contest – over 66 years to be exact. It's watched by millions of viewers worldwide every year; an annual tradition for us Europeans, that leaves the rest of the world somewhat scratching their heads. But despite its bizarre nature, the overarching message of love, peace and unity has always been prevalent. It's even inspired a movie.

Let's be honest with ourselves though, we are a *little* obsessed with it. We treasure it for its excess: the eccentric costumes, the extravagant staging, the comical commentary (the memes!) – we adore it because it's the definition of *extra*. The Eurovision Song Contest is exhilarating, fun, joyful and more than a bit bonkers, but most of all, it's unashamedly, pop!

It is also a great reason to throw party if you ever really needed an excuse! It's motivation to *Rise Like a Phoenix* and celebrate with our friends and family (and the rest of Europe) — whether it's an intimate watch party or, like the show itself, an elaborate soirée that's on the right side of nutty.

So, get your party hat on. It's Eurovision time. The excitement and the cringe of the world's most ridiculous song contest is about to hit you at warp speed. And I am so here for it.

PERFECT PERFORMANCE

What *is* the perfect performance, I hear you shout? Ever since the first Eurovision Song Contest, way back in 1956, the competition has delivered a platform for the best (and the weirdest) that pop music has to offer. It is the world's most famous song contest for a reason. So here I have humbly assembled seven *essential* steps to help you deliver an irresistible performance.

Phase 1: Staging. Grab the audience's attention with a powerful and theatrical start. Make it dramatic. Think flashing laser lights, ostentatious choreography, Cirque du Soleil-style acrobatics, or (a lot of the time *and*) fireworks.

Phase 2: Percussion! Never forget the mighty drum.

Phase 3: Show the audience (and the millions watching at home) your country's culture by using an obscure traditional instrument that no one's heard of before. The odder, the better.

Phase 4: In Eurovision, nothing screams champion like a violin solo. Trust me, it's a must-bring.

Phase 5: Jazzing up the antiquated instruments with a DJ who scrubs – or at least fakes it. This will give your performance that *fresh* feel; trust in the process.

Phase 6: Costumes! You need to look striking. Something that will make the viewers sit up and gasp. Sparkly spandex comes in handy here.

Phase 7: The song. The song is crucial! It needs to give the audience all the feels, with a catchy hook. Power ballads of unrequited or lost love is a sure fire way to go. Songs about world peace works too.

Now that you have everything you need, go for it. Wind machines at ready. Set. Go! May the odds be ever in your favour.

NIL POINTS, DOUZE POINTS!

Trivia & Challenges

EUROVISION QUIZ

Let's get the festivities started with a friendly round of trivia. And what better way to kick off the evening's entertainment, than on a competitive note? A trivia quiz is a lively social game; it's interactive and great at rallying the young, old and everyone in between. Whether in teams, or individually, nothing compares to the challenge of remembering completely unimportant facts or the joy of proving a teammate wrong when your correct answer is announced.

Over the following pages you'll find some excellent (if I do say so myself) Euro-centric questions primed for just such an occasion. However, since Eurovision has been on our screens for over 60 years, if you wanted to assemble your own set of trivia questions, there's a plethora of resources out there and practically eons of weird and wonderful facts up for grabs.

Let's get to the nitty-gritty. How much do you know about the annual singing competition? Can you avoid nil points? Knowledge is power, and (as we all know) with great power comes the great responsibility of making sure everyone knows you're smarter than they are! So, what are you waiting for?

ROUND 1: EUROPE

1. Which European country comes first, alphabetically?

2. In which country can you find the Westernmost point of Mainland Europe?

3. How many countries use the Euro?

4. Which is the most densely populated country in Europe?

5. What is the longest river in Europe?

6. What is the capital of Bulgaria?

7. Which countries does the Czech Republic share borders with?

8. Which is the largest island in the Mediterranean Sea?

9. Which country's parliament is called the Storting?

10. Which European country restored its monarchy in 1975?

ROUND 2: EUROVISION SONG CONTENT

1. How many countries entered the first ever Eurovision Song Contest in 1956?

2. And which country won that first year?

3. Which country has won the most Eurovision Song Contests?

4. Which country holds the record for finishing second?

5. In which year did Graham Norton take over from Terry Wogan in the commentary box?

6. How old was Eurovision's youngest ever winner?

7. How many times has Germany won the Eurovision Song Contest?

8. Céline Dion won the Eurovision Song Contest in 1988, but for which country?

9. What African country (the only one ever) made its debut at the Eurovision Song Contest in 1980?

10. At the Champion of Champions contest in Copenhagen in 2005, what was voted the best Eurovision song of all time?

ROUND 3: PICTURE ROUND, FLAGS OF EUROPE

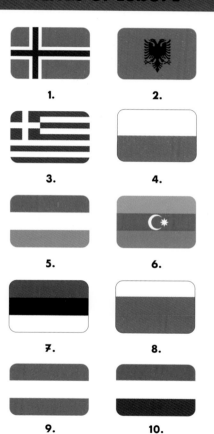

1.

2.

3.

4.

5.

6.

7.

8.

9.

10.

FINISH THE LYRICS

This game really is as simple as it sounds – just fill in the missing words to the lyrics. But have you ever really paid attention to your favourite Eurovision song? Can you remember the lyrics? Simply put, will you be able to rise to the challenge? This game will certainly distinguish the experts from the wannabes.

Ready for a trip down memory lane?

1. Waterloo/ I was defeated, you won the war/ Waterloo/ Promise to _____

2. Fly on the wings of love/ Fly, baby, fly/ Reaching _____

3. (Ooh Aah) A little bit more/ (Ooh Aah) Just a little bit/ I'll give you love _____

4. Come closer, come closer and listen/ the beat of my heart _____

5. Love, my aim is straight and true/ Cupid's arrow is _____

6. And now you really gotta burn it up/ And make another_____

FINISH THE LYRICS

7. Out of the ashes seeking rather than vengeance/
Retribution _____

8. I'm in love with a fairytale/ Even though it hurts/
'Cause I don't care _____

9. Euphoria/ Forever, 'til the end of time/ From
now on _____

10. Like the mighty river, flowing from the stream/ Let
our love shine a light _____

GUESS THE SONG

This Eurovision version of the game Guess the Song is much like the music round of a pub quiz. Play the first 20 seconds of a famous Eurovision song and your guests get points or prizes for guessing what it is! Easy peasy, right? If you want to make it extra tricky, just reduce the listening time. Here's a short list to get you started:

* *Heroes* Måns Zelmerlöw 2015

* *Hard Rock Hallelujah* Lordi 2006

* *Rise Like a Phoenix* Conchita Wurst 2014

* *Puppet on a String* Sandie Shaw 1967

* *Ne Partez Pas Sans Moi* Céline Dion 1987

* *Save Your Kisses for Me* Brotherhood of Man 1976

* *Diva* Dana International 1998

* *Nel Blu* Dipinto di Blu Domenico Modugno 1958

* *1944* Jamala 2016

* *Space Man* Sam Ryder 2022

GUESS THE YEAR

Do you think you know your Lordi from your ABBA? Now's the time to show off. Test your Eurovision knowledge, with a titillating game of Guess the Year. Simply select one person to be quiz master (a sparkly quiz master jacket always come in handy); they have to call out a song or famous contender, and your contestants must guess which year the song or contender featured in. Make it as simple or dastardly difficult as you like. Here are some particularly tricky suggestions from the last ten years:

Song	Artist	Country	Year
Not the Same	Sheldon Riley	Australia	2022
Tick-Tock	Albina	Croatia	2021
The Best in Me	Tom Leeb	France	2020
Like It	Zena	Belarus	2019
Higher Ground	Rasmussen	Denmark	2018
Breathlessly	Claudia Faniello	Malta	2017
Miracle	Samra	Azerbaijan	2016
Still in Love with You	Electro Velvet	UK	2015
Rise Like a Phoenix	Conchita Wurst	Austria	2014
Gravity	Zlata Ognevich	Ukraine	2013

IT'S ALL FUN AND GAMES!

⭐

Party Games

A party isn't a party without some games and shenanigans. Although we are here for it, the song contest can be pretty darn long once the show gets going – around 25 countries usually take part in the Grand Final, not to mention those who didn't take part, but will be casting their votes. So, some fun and lively party games are vital to keep things *Boom Bang-a-Bang* bouncy.

THE SWEEPSTAKE

Being the responsible party host that you are, you can appreciate that drinking games aren't for everybody. Thus, in the interest of inclusivity, here's a gambling game instead. Sweepstakes are a delightful way to get behind a country and root for them to do well.

The rules of a sweepstake are quite simple: each participant picks a competing country at random (out of a party hat to keep things traditional, or an opaque container so there's no peeking as they pick), until all the countries have been chosen. Et voila! The winner is the jammy person who picked the country that wins the contest. And all you really have to do to prepare is pop folded pieces of paper with the country's name written on it, into said hat or hat-like vessel.

What's the winning prize? Players can put an agreed amount into a kitty as the prize before the countries are picked, and the winner can smugly walk away with all the cash. However, if you don't want to gamble, you could always consider a trophy, or a gold star for a prize, with all bragging rights included, free of charge.

BINGO

✳

Clutch your dibbers, dabbers and daubers, and mark off the items on your bingo card as the performers… well, perform.

For those of you needing a quick reminder – all you have to do is cross off a point on your premade bingo card every time something on your card happens on screen during the show. Scream, yell or obnoxiously dance if you manage to get every item. The rules are very much up to you – you can win prizes by covering a complete horizontal, vertical or diagonal line. Or only give them out for the victorious full house.

Warning! You may need to referee on those tough calls. Was that a cheeky wink to camera? Or was it glitter in the eye from the cannon? With great power comes great responsibility, you know.

Making your own bingo cards couldn't be simpler, just fill out each box with things you would expect to see on the night. The list is endless, but here are some great examples:

THE SHOW

UK receives 'douze points'

Graham Norton makes a sly comment

The presenters change outfits

Terry Wogan is mentioned

Awkward long pause

A presenter sings for absolutely no reason

Flagrant political voting

Technical glitch

This isn't a European country!

Someone mentions ABBA

Cringey joke from presenters

Graham Norton gets the giggles

THE STAGE

Glitter cannon

Wind machine

Performer crying happy tears

Excessive use of smoke machine

Fake playing of an instrument

Power note held way too long

Gratuitous use of the violin or accordion

Semi-naked dancers

Singer kneels on stage

Wardrobe malfunction

Autotune level 100

Circus performers

THE PERFORMANCE

Double key change in one song

Traditional dress

Song about world peace

Fake rain

Mid-song costume change

Children singing

'Subtle' wink to camera

Awkward rapping

Edgy barefoot singing

Zany choreography

So much sequins

Pole dancing

CHARADES

Charades! Tremendously fun and lively, and absolutely everyone can join in – it's a classic for a reason. You really can't go wrong with a quick game of charades with a Eurovision twist, so brush up on your pantomiming skills.

If you don't already know; divide into teams, and each team should take it in turns for one person to draw a prompt and act out – without speaking – what is written. It could be a famous person, a musical act, a country, a song or even words and phrases generally related to Eurovision (duh!). Just as with the sweepstake – all you have to do to prepare is pop folded pieces of paper with the answer written on it, into a bowl or hat.

Teammates have one minute to correctly guess the answer. If your team fails to get it right, the play passes to the opposing team; they can confer and have one chance to steal the point from you. The first team to score ten points wins.

Actions

* Song: pretend to sing

* Phrases & words: make air quotes with fingers

* Person or Act: stand with hands on hips

* Country: make a circle with one hand, then point to it, as if pointing to a dot on a map

CHARADES

Common gestures

* Number of words: hold up the corresponding number of fingers.

* The word you are working on: hold up the number of fingers again.

* Number of syllables in the word: lay the number of fingers on your arm.

* Someone has guessed part of the charade correctly: point at your nose with one hand, while pointing at the person with your other hand.

Examples:

* Song: *Space Man* Sam Ryder 2022

* Phrase/word: Nil Points!

* Person/act: Conchita Wurst

* Country: Italy

WHO AM I?

Nothing like a deductive reasoning game to stir a little casual competition between you and your friends! The game of DIY Who Am I allows you to live out your glorious dreams of being Sherlock Holmes or Poirot.

Simply write down an undisclosed Eurovision-related individual on a piece of paper or sticky note and stick it to your neighbouring player's forehead. That person will then try to guess who they are by asking questions (to which everyone else can only reply 'yes', or 'no') in order to work out who they are.

GRAHAM NORTON

KATRINA AND THE WAVES

ABBA

CÉLINE DION

LOREEN

MÅNESKIN

JEDWARD

JAMALA

CORRY BROKKEN

PETRA MEDE

CONCHITA WURST

GINA G

PIN THE ARTIST

An oldie, but a goodie. You can't get more classic than a game of pin the tail on the donkey… well, a mic on the artist in this case. It's been played for generations, and be honest with yourself: no party is truly complete without it.

You can always buy ready-made kits for the game, however, it's just as easy to print out mini mics and a poster-sized picture of your favourite Eurovision artist to stick on a wall. But if you're feeling a little extra, just channel your inner Blue Peter and create your very own design for everyone to ooh and aah over.

Make sure you create enough mics for every partaker and write their names on it – nobody wants the fun police to make an appearance.

Everyone knows the rules – stick a cut-out image of an artist (ideally showing them holding a mic!) to the wall, blindfold someone, place the paper mic in their hand, give them a good spin and nudge them towards the cut-out. The player that gets the mic closest to the artist's hand, wins.

PASS THE PARCEL

You may think that this game is just for kids, but think again! Embrace your inner child and play a game of pass the parcel.

All you need to do is wrap a prize in several layers of paper (pointless and silly novelty items work best here) and press play on your favourite Eurovision playlist. The idea is to pass around the many-layer-wrapped parcel with the prize inside, while the song is playing. When the music stops, one layer should be unwrapped, and the parcel passed along when the music starts again, until the surprise in the final layer is reached.

Why not add a cheeky dare or a little spicy forfeit in each layer – that'll keep everyone on their toes.

MUSICAL CHAIRS

Musical chairs is a must! If you're sceptical, fear not! A game of musical chairs is still a strong favourite for many people. Chances are that your friends will absolutely love it and thoroughly enjoy themselves, especially after a few cocktails.

Set up two lines of chairs back-to-back. Make sure there is one less chair than there are people and that there is nothing breakable nearby. Have your playlist ready. Oh and don't forget a camera – you are going to want some pictures of this carnage.

Get everyone to form a circle around the chairs. When the music starts, have everyone walk (or dance!) around the chairs. When the music stops, everyone has to jump onto a chair. The one person left standing, is out. Remove another chair and continue until only one person is left. That's it. It's that simple… fun though.

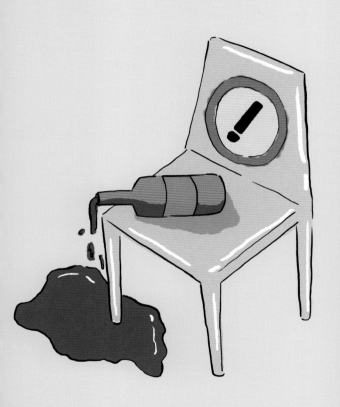

CROWN YOUR VERY OWN WINNER (SCORECARDS)

We know what we like, and we know what we don't like. Sure, our criteria may not quite line up with the official judges, but that's the beauty. We can be our very own judge.

EUROVISION FINALISTS	Catchiness (Song)	On Point (Choreography)	Dusted (Staging, outfits & props)	Eleganza Extravaganza (Performance)	Wild Card (Element of surprise)	Total
	0-10	0-10	0-10	0-10	0-10	
Australia						
Azerbaijan						
Belgium						
Bulgaria						
Cyprus						
Czech Republic						
France						
Germany						
Greece						
Israel						
Italy						
Lithuania						
Moldova						

Award your marks out of ten for each unique category and add the totals to give each act a score out of 50. Be sure to compare your results with friends!

EUROVISION FINALISTS	Catchiness (Song)	On Point (Choreography)	Dusted (Staging, outfits & props)	Eleganza Extravaganza (Performance)	Wild Card (Element of surprise)	Total
	0-10	0-10	0-10	0-10	0-10	
Netherlands						
Norway						
Portugal						
Bulgaria						
Serbia						
Spain						
Sweden						
Ukraine						
United Kingdom						

DRINKING GAMES

This can make or break your gatherings, but there's nothing quite like a drinking game or two to liven up a party. A tradition that's almost as rich as the contest itself, what better way is there to celebrate the unforgettable sequinned performances, than with a good old knees up?

When I think of drinking games, my mind always blazes back to a reliable game of Ring of Fire (cue bleary flashbacks), the cornerstone of student nights. And while Ring of Fire is a dependable choice, there are truly only so many times you can force people to drink from the King cup. With that in mind, over the next few pages are some alternative drinking games to try out with your friends and family.

Oh, please do remember to be responsible, there's always that one friend who inevitably ends up getting loaded into a taxi home before the voting section even starts. You can play with alcohol or a soft drink. It's the taking part that counts!

Slammer Time:

Down a shot for each of the following:

* If someone fails to hit the High C

* Somebody winks at the camera

* If the audience applause lasts longer than ten seconds

* Someone forgets their words

* Wardrobe malfunction

* Somebody reading out the jury votes is wearing feathers

* The UK gets 12 points from a jury vote

* If someone uses fireworks

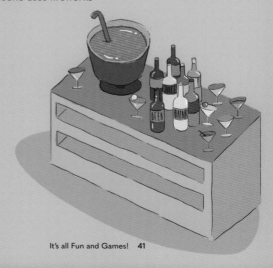

Boozy Bingo

Simply drink (or take a large gulp) whenever you cross something off the below list:

* Glitter cannon
* Anytime a wind machine is turned on
* If a contestant strips off a part of their costume
* Key change
* Whenever someone cries
* Verka Serduchka
* Clappy bit
* Someone throws a peace sign

International Drinking Rules

This game requires skill and memory – something that's slightly harder when you're a little bit tipsy. All you have to do is carry on socialising and watching the contest, but with a few added rules. If you are spotted breaking the rules, you see-off your drink, and if you don't break the rules, you win at being sober. Which would you prefer?

* No pointing

* No saying the words 'drink', 'drinking' or 'drunk'

* Only use a non-dominant hand for all single-handed tasks

* Always keep the pinky finger extended when drinking

* A glass cannot be put down empty, it must be refilled

* No calling a player by their first name

* No swearing

* No double-parking of drinks, if you are in possession of two drinks – one must be seen-off

TURN
IT UP

✦

Party Tunes

YOUR
EUROVISION
PLAYLIST

What's a Eurovision party without a thumping Eurovision playlist? From Bucks Fizz and Loreen to the iconic superstars that are ABBA, the contest has given us some of the world's greatest pop anthems, and may that gravy train never stop.

I know, I know, bizarrely not everyone enjoys the songs – ludicrous, right? But I have tempted and swayed many a nay-sayer in my time and this playlist of tried and trusted Eurovision party bangers will get your guests on the dancefloor. Douze points all round!

EURO-POP BOPS

Giorgos Alkaios and Friends – *Opa!*

Eric Saade – *Popular*

Ivi Adamou – *La La Love*

Anggun – *Echo (You and I)*

Eleni Foureira – *Fuego*

Alyona Lanskaya – *Solayoh*

Paula Seling and Ovi – *Miracle*

Pollapönk – *No Prejudice*

Nadav Guedj – *Golden Boy*

Barei – *Say Yay!*

Poli Genova – *If Love Was A Crime*

Ilinca feat. Alex Florea – *Yodel It!*

EUROVISION GEMS

Loreen – *Euphoria*

Dschinghis Khan – *Genghis Khan*

Lordi – *Hard Rock Hallelujah*

ABBA – *Waterloo*

Sertab Erener – *Everyway That I Can*

Emmelie De Forest – *Only Teardrops*

Jessy Matador – *Allez Ola Olé*

Conchita Wurst – *Rise Like a Phoenix*

LT United – *We Are the Winners*

Verka Serduchka – *Dancing Lasha Tumbai*

Morena – *Vodka*

Robin Bengtsoon – *I Can't Go On*

MOST PLAYED

Duncan Laurence – *Arcade*

Lena – *Satellite*

Mahmood – *Soldi*

Teach-In – *Ding-A-Dong*

Anne-Marie David – *Tu Tu Reconnaîtras*

Domenico Modugno – *Nel Blu Dipinto Di Blu*

Dana International – *Diva*

Alexander Rybak – *Fairytale*

ABBA – *Waterloo*

Måneskin – *Zitti E Buoni*

Mocedades – *Eres Tú*

Bucks Fizz – *Making Your Mind Up*

KARAOKE

Don't just leave the singing to the contestants on the show! Eurovision and karaoke go hand in hand like spandex and glitter. The songs are usually catchy and quick which makes them perfect for the karaoke slice of your party – and you'll be surprised at how eager everyone will be to have a go once they've had a couple of bevvies.

If you're still feeling a tiny bit competitive, why not have some of your guests as critics and they can channel their inner Simon Cowell and judge the best karaoke act. The winner has bragging rights... for at least a year.

BON APPÉTIT

Snacks & Libations

FOOD

When it comes to party food, European-themed nibbles will always be a hit. No matter how far we delve into the drama and spectacle of it all, the Eurovision Song Contest is a celebration of culture, customs and identity. What better time is there to whip up something in the kitchen that pays tribute to European diversity?

So, let your taste buds take you on a journey across the smörgåsbord of Europe and indulge in some of the most traditional and quintessentially European dishes and delicacies.

Keeping it light and casual – here are some bitesize, theme-appropriate munchies to sink your teeth into:

 Mini croque monsieurs

 Swedish meatballs

 Lamingtons

 Mini spanakopita (Greek spinach pies)

 Bruschetta

 Mini sandwich triangles

 Chorizo bites

 Mini curry-wurst

 Chouquettes or gougères

 Pierogi

 Pastéis de Nata

Frites

 Falafel & hummus

 Toast skagen

 Patatas bravas with garlic aioli

 Mini victoria sponges

 Kalamata olives and lesvos feta

 Black forest brownies or cupcakes

 Shards of hokey pokey (honeycomb)

 Khachapuri (cheese-filled bread)

 Halloumi skewers

 Stroopwafel

DRINKS

Go grab yourself some swanky French wine, some premium Polish vodka, Swiss schnapps, a few bottles of Italian Prosecco, or maybe even some Spanish sangria. Give a nod to Australia's participation with some tinnies of Fosters, et viola! You've got yourself a well-stocked European bar. Fancy really pushing the boat out? Here are a few cocktail ideas to give the evening an extra pinch of pizazz.

BLUE LAGOON

Makes 2
Glasses: 2 highball glasses
Equipment: Cocktail shaker, strainer

2 measures blue curaçao

2 measures vodka

juice of 1 lemon

juice of 1 orange

juice of 1 lime

100ml soda water

4 maraschino cherries and 1 teaspoon of the syrup

cracked ice

Half-fill a cocktail shaker with ice cubes, and put the rest into each highball glass. Pour over the curaçao, vodka, fruit juices and syrup from the cherries. Stir until frost forms on the outside of the shaker. Strain over the ice in the glass and serve.

PIÑA COLADA

Makes 2
Glasses: 2 highball glasses
Equipment: Food processor

2 measures white rum

4 measures coconut cream

4 measures pineapple juice

crushed ice

pineapple leaves, to decorate

orange slices, to decorate

Put the white rum, coconut cream and pineapple juice into a food processor with some crushed ice and blend. Transfer to 2 large highball glasses, decorate with pineapple leaves and orange slices and serve.

SEX ON THE BEACH

Makes 2
Glasses: 2 highball glasses
Equipment: Cocktail shaker, strainer

ice cubes

2 measures vodka

2 measures peach schnapps

2 measures cranberry juice

2 measures orange juice

2 measures pineapple juice (optional)

lemon and lime wedges, to decorate

Put 8–10 ice cubes into a cocktail shaker and add the vodka, schnapps, cranberry juice, orange juice and pineapple juice (if used). Shake well. Put 3–4 ice cubes into each highball glass, strain over the cocktail and decorate with the lemon and lime wedges.

TEQUILA SUNRISE

Makes 2
Glasses: 2 highball glasses
Equipment: Food processor

2 teaspoons grenadine

4 measures tequila

8 measures fresh orange juice

ice cubes

orange slices, to decorate

Put 5–6 ice cubes in a cocktail shaker, add tequila and fresh orange juice and shake to mix. Strain into 2 highball glasses over plenty of ice, then slowly pour the grenadine into each one, allowing it to settle. Decorate each glass with an orange slice.

COSMOPOLITAN

Makes 2
Glasses: 2 chilled martini glasses
Equipment: Cocktail shaker, strainer

2 measures vodka

1 measure Cointreau

2 measures cranberry juice

juice of 1 lime

cracked ice

orange twists, to decorate (optional)

Pour all the ingredients into a shaker with some cracked ice. Shake and double strain into chilled martini glasses, and decorate with orange twists, if you like, and serve.

HARVEY WALLBANGER

Makes 2
Glasses: 2 rocks glasses
Equipment: Cocktail shaker, strainer

2 teaspoons Galliano

4 measures vodka

6 measures orange juice

cracked ice

Half-fill a cocktail shaker with ice cubes and put 6–8 ice cubes into each old-fashioned glass. Add all the remaining ingredients to the shaker and shake until a frost forms on the outside of the shaker. Strain over the ice in the glasses and serve.

DRESS IT UP!

Fancy Dress & Decorations

FANCY DRESS

Okay, this may be one for the hardcore fans, and admittedly I am yet to dress up as Lordi or Jedward. But what's a themed party without fancy dress? A Eurovision party can never be too over the top.

The show itself is a mix of glitter and sparkles, red carpet glam, and a whole lot of feathers. The object of the contest is to unite different countries in their common love of pure entertainment – the bigger and brighter, the better. That's what Eurovision is all about. So, take my advice and make the most of all the glitz and sparkle, and go all out in true extravagant Eurovision style.

Here are some iconic outfits to help get those creative juices flowing:

ABBA

Grab three other friends and transform yourselves into Anni-Frid, Agnetha, Björn and Benny. Maybe it's a subtle nod with a pair of white flares – or better yet, knickerbockers! Bow down and pay tribute to the greatest of all time.

JEDWARD

Love them or hate them, you will never forget them. Jedward and Eurovision are a marriage made in heaven. Coordinate with a mate and don a tall Jedward-style wig, and you're halfway there.

VERKA SERDUCHKA

The Ukrainian comedian Andriy Danylko channelled his inner queen in this spectacular outfit. Verka may have come second, but she shines like the star she is.

LORDI

Why not emulate the heavy-metal winners from Finland by wearing a scary monster mask? Pull the look together with some fitted pleather trousers, studs and chains. Finish your look with a black cape, and you'll be rocking the Lordi-look in no time.

SCOOCH

Take to the skies with kitschy blue flight attendant-style outfits. It's easy to replicate: a simple suit and jacket or fitted dress – add some white gloves and a jaunty little hat. The song may have been plane awful, but their look is certainly memorable.

CONCHITA

Bring out your inner diva! Dress up as one of the most iconic winners in recent years. Throw on a statement gown, some killer heels, blowout your hair and don a paper beard mask (or real facial hair will do the trick).

Still stuck? Try these for size:

* Dressing as a national flag is one of the easiest ways to dress up and support your favourite Eurovision contestant's country. Throw on some face paint and you got yourself a look.

* If you're supporting the UK, the infamous Union Jack dress costume will definitely add some *Girl Power* to your party.

* Pay tribute to the costume of the 2002 Netherlands entrant, Linda Wagenmaker. She wore a ginormous circus tent skirt on stage. She certainly got the memo that bigger is better.

* Do-it-yourself with some coloured card and a stapler or better yet a traffic cone, for Moldova's Zdob şi Zdub's garden gnome look.

* Feel like getting your legs out on the night? Team a crisp white shirt, black tie, and some sequinned hotpants and what you have is Inculto, Lithuania's 2010 entry. Oh, and fabulous!

* If you're still struggling, or just want to take the easy route, why not come dressed as one of the participating countries? For example: Germany, think lederhosen, a beret for France or a flamenco dress for Spain. Olé!

DECKING THE HALLS

✦

This all may depend on your own personal level of extra (mine is pretty high). Flag-themed bunting is a reliable no-brainer – you can squeeze in a little geography lesson as a bonus.

Recreate some of the magic of the stage by hanging twinkly lights. Balloons, streamers and a healthy sprinkling of confetti will also add a lovely touch, and if it feels too much, add some more – though I take no responsibility for the clean up after!

Here's an idea: cover your darling family photos up with the image of an iconic Eurovision act! Forget your wedding snaps, pop a picture of Céline Dion in instead. Those baby pictures are really cute, but Dana International is more of a talking point!

Why not kick it up a notch and designate a 'photo booth' area for some amusing selfies. Simply find a space, a chair, some lighting and hang a backdrop. Oh, and don't forget to pop on some playful props. Inflatable mics, wigs, novelty glasses and masks are pretty much all you need. See? Easy-peasy (ish).

Ever thought to add a glitter corner? Too much? Told you I was extra. A glitter station is guaranteed to be a popular zone, especially with those who want to jazz up their already excellent outfits. Get some colourful biodegradable face glitter and petroleum jelly and leave the rest to your guests.

You've now got yourself all the ingredients for some fantastic Eurovision memories.

Cheers!

AND THE AWARD GOES TO....

The Eurovision winner has been announced, you've indulged in one too many bratwursts, and your evening is slowly coming to a close (cue the cut-off music). But wait! You're not quite ready to hang up your glad-rags.

Glory and awards shouldn't just be held for Eurovision contestants on the telly. Get in on the action; everyone likes to be rewarded for their efforts, especially when it comes to reigning supreme over quizzes, busting some bomb moves on the dancefloor or for having the silliest costume.

End the evening on a high-note and get your Oscar-worthy speeches ready!

The categories are:

* **For the most snatched outfit:** they understood the assignment.

* **The sober award:** well, someone had to be...

* **Flawless karaoke skills:** seriously, why aren't you competing in the official contest?

* **Lyrical genius:** winner of the most songs memorised, is your brain a walking jukebox?

* **Human Wikipedia:** quiz champion! You have well-earned your bragging rights.

AND THE AWARD GOES TO....

* **The game slayer:** overall games gold-medallist. Wow, you're a competitive one!

* **Fierce jazzercize realness:** those were some strong moves you were throwing.

* **Celeb spotter:** knowing the most 'celebrities' representing their home countries. That is a keen eye!

* **Luck of the draw:** congrats, you won the sweepstake; you get the cash and a prize. Some people have all the luck!

* **Nil point hero:** so, your chosen country didn't win any points. At least you have something to show for it...

THE WINNER TAKES IT ALL

The Winners and Losers

THE BEST OF THE BEST

We all know, that ABBA are the best when it comes to Eurovision greatness. But over the years, Eurovision has given the world some outstanding cheesy pop classics. Here are ten of the highest scoring winners at the grand finale.

* **758 Points** – Salvador Sobral, *Amar pelos dois* – Portugal, 2017

* **631 Points** – Kalush Orchestra, *Stefania* – Ukraine, 2022

* **615 Points** – Kristian Kostov, *Beautiful Mess* – Bulgaria, 2017

* **534 Points** – Jamala, *1944* – Ukraine, 2016

* **529 Points** – Netta, *Toy* – Israel, 2018

* **524 Points** – Måneskin, *Zitti e Buoni* – Italy, 2021

* **511 Points** – Dami Im, *Sound of Silence* – Australia, 2016

* **499 Points** – Barbara Pravi, *Voilà* – France, 2021

* **498 Points** – Duncan Laurence, *Arcade* – Netherlands, 2019

* **472 Points** – Mahmood, *Soldi* – Italy, 2019

Special mention:

* **466 Points** – Sam Ryder, *Space Man* – UK, 2022

THE BEST OF THE WORST

A dreaded experience that any act fears to hear, after the lengthy ordeal of sitting through the voting, country by country. It's a fine line that separates fame from shame at Eurovision, and to date there are only 37 victims to score zilch. Here are last the ten entrants to come away with nil points, and there some repeat offenders.

* **2021** United Kingdom – James Newman, *Embers*

* **2015** Austria – The Makers, *I Am Yours*

* **2015** Germany – Ann Sophie, *Black Smoke*

* **2003** United Kingdom – Jemini, *Cry Baby*

* **1998** Switzerland – Gunvor Guggisbers, *Lass' ihn*

* **1997** Norway – Tor Endresen, *San Francisco*

* **1997** Portugal – Célia Lawson, *Antes do Adeus*

* **1994** Lithuania – Ovidijus Vyšniauskas, *Lopšinė mylimai*

* **1991** Austria – Thomas Forstner, *Venedig im Regen*

* **1989** Iceland – Daníel Ágúst Haraldsson, *Það sem enginn sér*

ANSWERS

Eurovision Quiz

Europe: 1. Albania **2.** Portugal **3.** 19 **4.** Monaco **5.** Volga **6.** Sofia **7.** Germany, Poland, Austria, Slovakia, **8.** Sicily **9.** Norway **10.** Spain

Eurovision Song Contest: 11. Seven **12.** Switzerland **13.** Ireland (seven times) **14.** UK (15 times) **15.** 2009 **16.** Thirteen **17.** Twice (1982 & 2010) **18.** Switzerland **19.** Morocco **20.** Waterloo (ABBA, 1974)

Flags of Europe: 1. Norway **2.** Albania **3.** Greece **4.** Poland **5.** Luxembourg **6.** Azerbaijan **7.** Estonia **8.** Bulgaria **9.** Austria **10.** Netherlands

Finish the Lyrics

1. 'love you forever' *Waterloo* (ABBA, 1974) **2.** 'the stars above' *Fly on the Wings of Love* (The Olsen Brothers, 2000) **3.** 'you can't ignore' *Ooh Aah... Just a Little Bit* (Gina G, 1996) **4.** 'keeps on missing' *Boom Bang a Bang* (Lulu, 1969) **5.** 'just for you' *Satellite* (Lena, 2010) **6.** 'fly by night' *Making Your Mind Up* (Bucks Fizz, 1981) **7.** 'you were warned' *Rise Like a Phoenix* (Conchita Wurst, 2014) **8.** 'if I lose my mind' *Fairytale* (Alexander Rybak, 2009) **9.** 'only you and I' *Euphoria* (Loreen, 2012) **10.** 'in every corner of my dreams' *Love Shine a Light* (Katrina and the Waves, 1997)